# THE OFFICIAL

# Arsenal

# ANNUAL 2016

*Dear Sundeep,*
*You ma boi*
*Yours tru-*
*G,*

**Written by Josh James**
**Designed by Jon Dalrymple**

A Grange Publication

ISBN 978-1-910199-39-8

# Contents

# Manager's Message

Dear supporter,

Welcome to the Official Arsenal Annual 2016.

Last season was another memorable campaign for the club.

We ended it with an unforgettable day at Wembley, lifting the FA Cup after a very satisfying win over Aston Villa. It's always a big achievement to win the FA Cup, and to retain it is even more difficult, so we are very proud of what we managed.

Of course we were delighted to win another trophy, but - just like the fans - my players and I want more.

I believe we have built a very strong squad that is capable of challenging for all the honours this season. That is our aim.

Players such as Alexis Sanchez and Mesut Ozil have fully adapted to the Premier League, our talented youngsters continue to develop every season, and we also have plenty of experience within the squad now. We have grown together, and we are up for the fight.

By bringing Petr Cech in the summer too, I think we have added an extra competitive edge. We are very strong in all areas of the pitch.

In this annual you can find out more about our squad for this season, remind yourself of the highlights from 2014/15 and hopefully have some fun too with the puzzles and quizzes.

True Arsenal fans like yourself are who the team depend upon each year to motivate us to greater triumphs. Your support means so much to us, and we hope that we will have many more successes and trophies to celebrate together over the coming seasons.

So thank you for your tremendous support, and hopefully we will see you at Emirates Stadium soon!

**Arsène Wenger – Manager**

## Roll Of Honour

| | |
|---|---|
| **League champions:** | 1931, 1933, 1934, 1935, 1938, 1948, 1953, 1971, 1989, 1991, 1998, 2002, 2004 |
| **FA Cup winners:** | 1930, 1936, 1950, 1971, 1979, 1993, 1998, 2002, 2003, 2005, 2014, 2015 |
| **League Cup winners:** | 1987, 1993 |
| **European Fairs Cup winners:** | 1970 |
| **European Cup Winners' Cup winners:** | 1994 |
| **Charity/Community Shield winners:** | 1930, 1931, 1933, 1934, 1938, 1948, 1953, 1991 (shared), 1998, 1999, 2002, 2004, 2014, 2015 |

# Season Review
## Community Shield

Arsenal kicked off season 2014/15 just how they had finished the previous campaign – and how they would complete this one – by lifting silverware at Wembley.

This time it was the Community Shield, against reigning champions Manchester City, and Arsène Wenger's men ran out convincing 3-0 victors.

Santi Cazorla, Aaron Ramsey and Olivier Giroud scored the goals on a day when five Gunners, including Alexis Sanchez, made their first-team debuts.

**Aug 10  Manchester City  N  3-0**
**Cazorla, Ramsey, Giroud**

# The Premier League

## August

The Premier League season got underway with a win - for the first time since 2009 - thanks to Aaron Ramsey's last-gasp goal at home to Crystal Palace. There was more late drama away to Everton - Ramsey was again on target, then Olivier Giroud headed home in injury-time to salvage a draw.

Alexis Sanchez netted his first Premier League goal in a 1-1 draw away to newly-promoted Leicester at the end of the month.

### Results

| | | |
|---|---|---|
| **Aug 16 Crystal Palace** | **H** | **2-1** |
| Koscielny, Ramsey | | |
| **Aug 23 Everton** | **A** | **2-2** |
| Ramsey, Giroud | | |
| **Aug 31 Leicester City** | **A** | **1-1** |
| Alexis | | |

## September

The unbeaten start to the season continued in September. Jack Wilshere and Alexis scored fine goals in a pulsating home draw with Manchester City before Aston Villa were brushed aside at Villa Park thanks to three goals in four first-half minutes. The month ended with Alex Oxlade-Chamberlain earning a late draw in the north London derby.

### Results

| | | |
|---|---|---|
| **Sept 13 Manchester City** | **H** | **2-2** |
| Wilshere, Alexis | | |
| **Sept 20 Aston Villa** | **A** | **3-0** |
| Ozil, Welbeck, Cissokho (og) | | |
| **Sept 27 Tottenham Hotspur** | **H** | **1-1** |
| Oxlade-Chamberlain | | |

FIAT

# Season Review
## The Premier League
### October

Defeat at Stamford Bridge was a blow, as was the home draw with Hull City that followed. But Danny Welbeck's late equaliser against the Tigers at least gave Arsenal some momentum, and a brace from Alexis – by now well into his stride in Arsenal colours – secured a comfortable win away to Sunderland at the end of the month.

## Results

| | | | |
|---|---|---|---|
| Oct 5 | Chelsea | A | 0-2 |
| Oct 18 | Hull City | H | 2-2 |
| Alexis, Welbeck | | | |
| Oct 25 | Sunderland | A | 2-0 |
| Alexis 2 | | | |

### November

The Alexis show continued apace in November. He claimed two, and defender Calum Chambers scored his first for the club, in a 3-0 win at home to Burnley. But then back-to-back defeats - against Swansea and Manchester United - rocked Arsenal. A thumping Welbeck header stopped the rot though with a narrow victory at The Hawthorns, to take the Gunners up to sixth position.

## Results

| | | | |
|---|---|---|---|
| Nov 1 | Burnley | H | 3-0 |
| Alexis 2, Chambers | | | |
| Nov 9 | Swansea City | A | 1-2 |
| Alexis | | | |
| Nov 22 | Manchester United | H | 1-2 |
| Giroud | | | |
| Nov 29 | West Bromwich Albion | A | 1-0 |
| Welbeck | | | |

# December

Another 1-0 win, this time courtesy of an 89th-minute Alexis strike against Southampton, kicked off December, but more disappointment followed at the Britannia Stadium.

Two goals each from Giroud and birthday-boy Cazorla put Arsenal back on track at home to Newcastle United, and only an injury-time equaliser denied the side what would have been an excellent win at Anfield.

However, a pair of 2-1 London derby triumphs, over QPR and West Ham, ensured Arsenal fans had plenty to cheer during the festive period.

## Results

| | | | |
|---|---|---|---|
| **Dec 3 Southampton** | H | 1-0 | |
| **Alexis** | | | |
| **Dec 6 Stoke City** | A | 2-3 | |
| **Cazorla, Ramsey** | | | |
| **Dec 13 Newcastle United** | H | 4-1 | |
| **Giroud 2, Cazorla 2** | | | |
| **Dec 21 Liverpool** | A | 2-2 | |
| **Debuchy, Giroud** | | | |
| **Dec 26 QPR** | H | 2-1 | |
| **Alexis, Rosicky** | | | |
| **Dec 28 West Ham United** | A | 2-1 | |
| **Cazorla, Welbeck** | | | |

# January

New Year's Day was marked with a disappointing result at high-flying Southampton but Arsenal soon turned fortunes around with a fine home win over Stoke City, which was followed a week later with an even more impressive showing away to champions Manchester City.

Cazorla - instrumental all afternoon at the Etihad Stadium - opened the scoring from the penalty spot, and Giroud sealed the win with a header. Arsenal were steadily climbing the table once more.

## Results

| | | |
|---|---|---|
| **Jan 1 Southampton** | A | 0-2 |
| **Jan 11 Stoke City** | H | 3-0 |
| **Koscielny, Alexis 2** | | |
| **Jan 18 Manchester City** | A | 2-0 |
| **Cazorla, Giroud** | | |

# Season Review
## The Premier League

### February

A five-star showing sent Villa packing at Emirates Stadium, but Arsenal's progress seemed to have been checked again with defeat at White Hart Lane, despite taking the lead against our local rivals. That game proved to be a turning point though, and a nervy 2-1 victory at home to Leicester kick-started an eight-game winning streak in the Premier League.

#### Results

| | | | |
|---|---|---|---|
| Feb 1 Aston Villa | H | 5-0 | |
| Giroud, Ozil, Walcott, Cazorla, Bellerin, | | | |
| Feb 7 Tottenham Hotspur | A | 1-2 | |
| Ozil | | | |
| Feb 10 Leicester City | H | 2-1 | |
| Koscielny, Walcott | | | |
| Feb 21 Crystal Palace | A | 2-1 | |
| Cazorla, Giroud | | | |

### March

Arsène Wenger was named Premier League manager of the month for March, after a clean sweep of victories. Giroud won the player of the month award too, after scoring in all four games. Home wins against Everton and West Ham sandwiched a gritty victory at QPR, and the Gunners continued their excellent form with a 2-1 win at St James' Park.

#### Results

| | | | |
|---|---|---|---|
| Mar 1 Everton | H | 2-0 | |
| Giroud, Rosicky | | | |
| Mar 4 QPR | A | 2-1 | |
| Giroud, Alexis | | | |
| Mar 14 West Ham United | H | 3-0 | |
| Giroud, Ramsey, Flamini | | | |
| Mar 21 Newcastle United | A | 2-1 | |
| Giroud 2 | | | |

# April

In one of the performances of the season, Arsenal blew away Liverpool at Emirates Stadium, thanks to three goals in eight minutes at the end of the first-half. Giroud crowned a perfect afternoon with a late fourth.

Ramsey's strike against Burnley was enough to bring up an eighth successive Premier League win, but Chelsea frustrated Wenger's men at home two weeks later to realistically end Arsenal's remaining title hopes.

## Results

**Apr 4 Liverpool H** 4-1
**Bellerin, Ozil, Alexis, Giroud**
**Apr 11 Burnley A** 1-0
**Ramsey**
**Apr 26 Chelsea H** 0-0

# May

Alexis was back on the goal trail in a highly entertaining 3-1 win at Hull City, a victory which all but secured Champions League football for the 18th consecutive season.

There was a shock defeat at home to Swansea a week later but Theo Walcott's late deflected goal at Old Trafford was enough to gain a point which consolidated Arsenal's third place.

After a midweek goalless draw with Sunderland, the Gunners rounded off the league campaign in style. Walcott scored a hat-trick and Wilshere thundered home a classic to beat West Brom 4-1.

## Results

**May 4 Hull City** A 3-1
**Alexis 2, Ramsey**
**May 11 Swansea City** H 0-1
**May 17 Manchester United** A 1-1
**Blackett (og)**
**May 20 Sunderland** H 0-0
**May 24 West Bromwich Albion** H 4-1
**Walcott 3, Wilshere**

## Game-by-game

| Game | League position |
|------|-----------------|
| 1 | 1 |
| 2 | 3 |
| 3 | 7 |
| 4 | 8 |
| 5 | 4 |
| 6 | 4 |
| 7 | 8 |
| 8 | 6 |
| 9 | 5 |
| 10 | 4 |
| 11 | 6 |
| 12 | 8 |
| 13 | 6 |
| 14 | 6 |
| 15 | 6 |
| 16 | 5 |
| 17 | 6 |
| 18 | 6 |
| 19 | 5 |
| 20 | 6 |
| 21 | 5 |
| 22 | 5 |
| 23 | 5 |
| 24 | 6 |
| 25 | 4 |
| 26 | 3 |
| 27 | 3 |
| 28 | 3 |
| 29 | 2 |
| 30 | 3 |
| 31 | 2 |
| 32 | 2 |
| 33 | 3 |
| 34 | 3 |
| 35 | 3 |
| 36 | 3 |
| 37 | 3 |
| 38 | 3 |

# Season Review
## The Champions League

Arsenal's Champions League campaign would eventually end in heartbreak, losing out to Monaco on the away goals rule, but there were plenty of highlights in another exciting campaign.

An Alexis Sanchez goal at Emirates Stadium - his first for the club - proved enough for Arsenal to see off Besiktas in the qualifier, and the side were safely through to the Champions League proper for the 17th season in a row.

The group stage got off to the worst possible start, with defeat in Dortmund, but Danny Welbeck's hat-trick at home to Galatasaray, and two dramatic, late goals in Belgium turned fortunes around. Yaya Sanogo scored his first for the club as qualification was assured with victory over Dortmund in London, and despite another 4-1 win over Galatasaray on the final matchday - including an unforgettable goal from Aaron Ramsey - Arsenal had to be content with second place in the group.

That meant a last-16 meeting with Arsène's Wenger's former club Monaco. Despite the optimism from fans and players alike, the French side shocked Arsenal in London, taking a 3-1 lead into the second leg.

Back in the Principality the Gunners put up a spirited and brave showing, roaring into a 2-0 lead, but for the second season in a row, the away goals rule proved their downfall.

## Qualifiers

| | | | | |
|---|---|---|---|---|
| Aug 19 | Besiktas | A | 0-0 | |
| Aug 27 | Besiktas | H | 1-0 | Alexis |

## Group stage

| | | | | |
|---|---|---|---|---|
| Sep 16 | Borrussia Dortmund | A | 0-2 | |
| Oct 1 | Galatasaray | H | 4-1 | Welbeck 3, Alexis |
| Oct 22 | Anderlecht | A | 2-1 | Gibbs, Podolski |
| Nov 4 | Anderlecht | H | 3-3 | Arteta, Alexis, Oxlade-Chamberlain |
| Nov 26 | Borrussia Dortmund | H | 2-0 | Sanogo, Alexis |
| Dec 9 | Galatasaray | A | 4-1 | Podolski 2, Ramsey 2 |

## Knock-out round

| | | | | |
|---|---|---|---|---|
| Feb 25 | AS Monaco | H | 1-3 | Oxlade-Chamberlain |
| Mar 17 | AS Monaco | A | 2-0 | Giroud, Ramsey |

Brief though it was, the Capital One Cup campaign was memorable for one thing - a stunning free-kick from Alexis Sanchez. Southampton had too much for a young Gunners side though, and progressed with a 2-1 Emirates Stadium win in the third round.

## Third Round

**Sept 23 Southampton   H   1-2**
**Alexis**

## Stats and facts

* Arsenal played 56 games in all competitions in 2014/15, winning 35

* Arsenal used 34 different players during the season, 21 of whom scored

* Nine players made their first-team debut during the season

* Santi Cazorla made the most appearances (53)

* Alexis Sanchez was the top scorer (25)

* 2-1 was the most common scoreline, recorded 10 times

# FA Cup Review

## Third Round
### Jan 4, 2015

**Arsenal 2 (Mertesacker, Alexis)**
**Hull City 0**

Arsenal's defence of the FA Cup started with a repeat of last season's final, though this game at Emirates Stadium was significantly lighter on drama than last May's showpiece. Per Mertesacker's header on 20 minutes settled any nerves, and Alexis Sanchez confirmed the win with eight minutes left, spinning on the edge of the box then beating Hull goalkeeper Steve Harper with a curling shot.

**FACT**

Arsenal have progressed past the FA Cup third round in each of the past 19 seasons

# Fourth Round
## Jan 25, 2015

**Brighton & Hove Albion 2 (O'Grady, Baldock)**
**Arsenal 3 (Walcott, Ozil, Rosicky)**

On a day of shocks in the FA Cup, Arsenal ensured their safe progression to the next round with a hard-fought win on the south coast. Theo Walcott's second-minute strike got things going, and the result seemed a formality when Mesut Ozil doubled the lead on 24 minutes. Brighton's Chris O'Grady then jolted Arsenal back into life early in the second half with a long-range strike, only for Tomas Rosicky to respond in style with a sumptuous 20-yard volley. Sam Baldock's goal ensured a nervy last 15 minutes, but the Gunners held on.

**FACT**
Arsenal beat Brighton away by the same score in the 2013 FA Cup

# Fifth Round
## Feb 15, 2015

**Arsenal 2 (Giroud 2)   Middlesbrough 0**

Two wonderful Olivier Giroud goals were enough to see off Championship high-fliers Middlesbrough at Emirates Stadium. The opener, on 27 minutes, was a typical 'Wengerball' goal. All 11 Arsenal players touched the ball in the build up, which was finished with a deft left-footed flick at the near post. Two minutes later Giroud reacted quickest to a left-wing corner to sweep home the second, and Arsenal were in control from that point on.

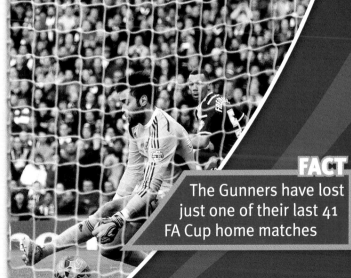

**FACT**
The Gunners have lost just one of their last 41 FA Cup home matches

# FA Cup Review

## Quarter-Final
### Mar 9, 2015

**Manchester United 1 (Rooney)  Arsenal 2 (Monreal, Welbeck)**

Danny Welbeck returned to his old stomping ground to knock Manchester United out of the FA Cup. It was the Gunners' first triumph at Old Trafford since 2006, as they took another huge stride towards retaining the FA Cup. Nacho Monreal was the unlikely scorer of the first goal, striding into the penalty area from left-back to finish expertly on 26 minutes. The lead lasted just three minutes though before Wayne Rooney levelled. Arsenal would have the final word on the hour mark, and almost inevitably it was Welbeck – who joined Arsenal from United in the summer – who scored it after pouncing on a stray backpass. Back to Wembley!

### FACT
This was Arsenal's 11th FA Cup quarter-final under Arsène Wenger, and 10th victory

# Semi-Final
## Apr 18, 2015

**Reading 1 (McCleary) Arsenal 2 (Alexis 2)**

Arsenal were far from their best against Championship side Reading at Wembley, but two goals from Alexis finally proved enough to book another final appearance. He looked to have put Arsenal firmly in control when he finished well from Ozil's sublime pass late in the first-half. Reading showed their battling spirit to level up, then continued to frustrate the Gunners, forcing the tie into extra-time. Alexis was the match-winner, though there was a huge slice of luck involved in the second goal. Just as thoughts were turning to a penalty shootout, the Chilean jinked his way into the box and squirmed a shot just under Royals' keeper Adam Federici, who failed to keep the ball out, despite a desperate dive on the line. So for the second time in 12 months, Arsenal were in the FA Cup final!

**FACT**

Arsenal set a new record for most appearances in the FA Cup semi-final - 28

# Final
## May 30, 2015

**Arsenal 4 (Walcott, Alexis, Mertesacker, Giroud) Aston Villa 0**

What a time and place to turn in one of the most complete team performances of the season. A day when, quite simply, every single Arsenal player rose to the occasion. The Gunners were hunting a record 12th FA Cup win, and were overwhelming favourites against Tim Sherwood's Villa. This was Arsenal's fourth FA Cup tie at Wembley in just over 12 months, but despite winning all three previous games, they hadn't reached their full potential in any of them. But there were to be no nerves this time, no stage fright as the footballing world looked on. Arsène Wenger's men surged forward from the first whistle, and the only surprise was how long the first goal took to arrive.

Walcott - given the nod up front over Giroud - scored it, five minutes before the break. He connected superbly with an Alexis knock down in the area to power in a left-footed volley. Five minutes after the restart Alexis scored his 25th goal of the season - a scorcher from 30 yards - to double the lead. The match was over as a contest when Mertesacker had a free header from a corner to make it 3-0 on the hour. Arsenal played keep ball after that, Wojciech Szczesny didn't have a serious save to make all evening, while his opposite number Shay Given was perhaps Villa's star performer. With seconds left Giroud flicked home Alex Oxlade-Chamberlain's cross at the near post to complete the rout - Arsenal's biggest ever FA Cup final win.

# Alexis Sanchez
## What a Season

Hopes were high among Gooners when Alexis Sanchez arrived from Barcelona in summer 2014, but surely even the most optimistic of Arsenal fans couldn't have anticipated the Chilean having such an incredible debut season in England.

His all-action, tenacious style of play was always going to endear himself to the Emirates faithful, but early on in his Gunners career he also demonstrated a keen eye for goal - and then he didn't stop finding the net all season. He broke his duck in the vital Champions League play-off victory over Besiktas at the end of August - a strike which triggered a run of 14 goals in 18 games. The Arsenal fans had a new hero to worship. He was duly voted Player of the Month for September, October and November by users of Arsenal.com.

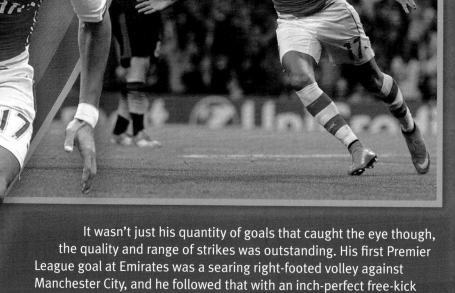

It wasn't just his quantity of goals that caught the eye though, the quality and range of strikes was outstanding. His first Premier League goal at Emirates was a searing right-footed volley against Manchester City, and he followed that with an inch-perfect free-kick against Southampton in the next home game. Individual goals, headers and poacher's efforts were all within his extensive repertoire.

# ALEXIS SANCHEZ GOALS 2014/15

| Date | Competition | Opposition | Venue | Score | Goals |
|------|-------------|------------|-------|-------|-------|
| 27/8/14 | Champions League | Besiktas | Home | 1-0 | 1 |
| 31/8/14 | Premier League | Leicester City | Away | 1-1 | 1 |
| 13/9/14 | Premier League | Manchester City | Home | 2-2 | 1 |
| 23/9/14 | Capital One Cup | Southampton | Home | 1-2 | 1 |
| 1/10/14 | Champions League | Galatasaray | Home | 4-1 | 1 |
| 18/10/14 | Premier League | Hull City | Home | 2-2 | 1 |
| 25/10/14 | Premier League | Sunderland | Away | 2-0 | 2 |
| 1/11/14 | Premier League | Burnley | Home | 3-0 | 2 |
| 4/11/14 | Champions League | Anderlecht | Home | 3-3 | 1 |
| 9/11/14 | Premier League | Swansea City | Away | 1-2 | 1 |
| 26/11/14 | Champions League | Borussia Dortmund | Home | 2-0 | 1 |
| 3/12/14 | Premier League | Southampton | Home | 1-0 | 1 |
| 26/12/14 | Premier League | QPR | Home | 2-1 | 1 |
| 4/1/15 | FA Cup | Hull City | Home | 2-0 | 1 |
| 11/1/15 | Premier League | Stoke City | Home | 3-0 | 2 |
| 4/3/15 | Premier League | QPR | Away | 2-1 | 1 |
| 4/4/15 | Premier League | Liverpool | Home | 4-1 | 1 |
| 18/4/15 | FA Cup | Reading | Wembley | 2-1 | 2 |
| 4/5/15 | Premier League | Hull City | Away | 3-1 | 2 |
| 30/5/15 | FA Cup | Aston Villa | Wembley | 4-0 | 1 |

When the big games came around at the end of the season, Alexis proved he was the man for the big occasion. A tremendous dipping long-range strike illuminated the 4-1 win over Liverpool in April and two weeks later he booked Arsenal's place in the FA Cup final with a brace against Reading at Wembley.

Alexis ended his season in the perfect manner in the final, scoring his 25th - and arguably best - goal of an unforgettable campaign. In fact it might even be described as Arsenal's best-ever FA Cup final goal.

He picked up possession more than 25 yards out while Nacho Monreal took away a defender with a clever overlap. Alexis didn't need a second invitation to shoot. He wound up his trusty right foot and arrowed a rocket over Shay Given and in off the cross bar.

"That was stunning - an absolute game changer," the beaten Aston Villa keeper said afterwards. "Sanchez has just produced a moment of sheer brilliance. The ball has moved all over the place and then off the bar. How are you supposed to get to that? He's a special player and that's what special players can do."

Special indeed. And now he's had 12 months to find his range, this season promises to be even better for the man from Chile...

# True or False?

Five of these weird and wonderful Arsenal facts are true, and five we have made up!

**1.** Theo Walcott was an extra in Lord of the Rings.  TRUE ☐  FALSE ☐

**2.** Kieran Gibbs has got a twin brother.  TRUE ☐  FALSE ☐

**3.** Mikel Arteta's wife starred in CSI Miami.  TRUE ☐  FALSE ☐

**4.** Mesut Ozil has got more than 20 million Twitter followers.  TRUE ☐  FALSE ☐

**5.** Jack Wilshere was born on New Year's Day.  TRUE ☐  FALSE ☐

**6.** David Ospina's brother-in-law is Real Madrid star James Rodriguez.  TRUE ☐  FALSE ☐

**7.** Alexis Sanchez owns seven dogs.  TRUE ☐  FALSE ☐

**8.** Laurent Koscielny once donated money to save an accordion factory in France.  TRUE ☐  FALSE ☐

**9.** Per Mertesacker has got 11 toes.  TRUE ☐  FALSE ☐

**10.** Gabriel was born in south London and moved to Brazil as a baby.  TRUE ☐  FALSE ☐

Answers on p61.

# Odd One Out

## Which is the odd one out in each of the following groups, and why?

1. Mathieu Debuchy, Olivier Giroud, Johan Djourou, Robert Pires, Patrick Vieira.

2. David Seaman, Bob Wilson, Manuel Almunia, Philippe Senderos, Jens Lehmann.

3. Robert Pires, Freddie Ljungberg, Theo Walcott, Dennis Bergkamp, Sol Campbell.

4. 2002, 2003, 2005, 2009, 2014.

5. Brighton, Middlesbrough, Manchester United, Reading, Tottenham.

6. Alan Smith, George Graham, Herbert Chapman, Bertie Mee, Arsène Wenger.

7. Dennis Bergkamp, William Gallas, Robin van Persie, Lee Dixon, Jack Wilshere.

8. Golden Gantry, North Bank, Clock End, Club Level, Diamond Club.

Answers on p61.

# Global Gunners

Players from 54 different countries have represented Arsenal Football Club. There have been 131 players in the club's history from outside the home nations of England, Scotland, Wales, Northern Ireland and Republic of Ireland - and they are all listed here.

Nelson Vivas

John Kosmina

Alex Manninger

Alexander Hleb

Thomas Verma

Silvinho

Lauren

Alexis Sanchez

David Ospina

Joel Campbell

Eduardo

Tomas Rosicky

Carlin Itonga

John Jensen

## 01 ARGENTINA (3)
Nelson Vivas
Fabian Caballero
Emiliano Martinez

## 02 AUSTRALIA (1)
John Kosmina

## 03 AUSTRIA (1)
Alex Manninger

## 04 BELARUS (1)
Alexander Hleb

## 05 BELGIUM (1)
Thomas Vermaelen

## 06 BRAZIL (8)
Silvinho
Edu
Juan
Gilberto
Julio Baptista
Denilson
Andre Santos
Gabriel

## 07 CAMEROON (2)
Lauren
Alexandre Song

## 08 CHILE (1)
Alexis Sanchez

## 09 COLOMBIA (1)
David Ospina

## 10 COSTA RICA (1)
Joel Campbell

## 11 CROATIA (2)
Davor Suker
Eduardo

## 12 CZECH REPUBLIC (3)
Michal Papadopulos
Tomas Rosicky
Petr Cech

## 13 DR CONGO (1)
Carlin Itonga

## 14 DENMARK (3)
John Jensen
Sebastian Svard
Nicklas Bendtner

## 15 ESTONIA (1)
Mart Poom

## 16 FRANCE (26)
Patrick Vieira
Remi Garde
Nicolas Anelka
Gilles Grimandi
Emmanuel Petit
David Grondin
Thierry Henry
Jeremie Aliadiere
Robert Pires
Sylvain Wiltord
Pascal Cygan
Gael Clichy
Mathieu Flamini
Abou Diaby
William Gallas
Bacary Sagna
Lassana Diarra
Samir Nasri
Mikael Silvestre
Francis Coquelin
Gilles Sunu
Laurent Koscielny
Sebastien Squillaci
Olivier Giroud
Yaya Sanogo
Mathieu Debuchy

## 17 GERMANY (10)
Alberto Mendez
Stefan Malz
Moritz Volz
Jens Lehmann
Per Mertesacker
Lukas Podolski
Serge Gnabry
Thomas Eisfeld
Mesut Ozil
Gedion Zelalem

## 18 GHANA (2)
Quincy Owusu-Abeyie
Emmanuel Frimpong

## 19 GREECE (1)
Stathis Tavlaridis

## 20 GUINEA (1)
Kaba Diawara

## 21 HOLLAND (7)
Gerry Keyser
Glenn Helder
Dennis Bergkamp
Marc Overmars
Gio van Bronckhorst
Robin van Persie
Nacer Barazite

## 22 ICELAND (3)
Albert Gudmundsson
Siggi Jonsson
Olafur Ingi Skulason

## 23 ISRAEL (1)
Yossi Benayoun

## 24 ITALY (2)
Arturo Lupoli
Vito Mannone

## 25 IVORY COAST (3)
Kolo Toure
Emmanuel Eboue
Gervinho

## 26 JAPAN (2)
Junichi Inamoto
Ryo Miyaichi

## 27 LATVIA (1)
Igors Stepanovs

## 28 LIBERIA (1)
Christopher Wreh

## 29 LIBYA (1)
Jehad Muntasser

## 30 LITHUANIA (1)
Tomas Danilevicius

## 31 MEXICO (1)
Carlos Vela

## 32 MOROCCO (1)
Marouane Chamakh

Mart Poom
 William Gallas
 Thomas Eisfeld
 Quincy Owusu-Abeyie
 Stathis Tavlaridis
 Kaba Diawara
 Glenn Helder

 Siggi Jonsson
 Yossi Benayoun
 Vito Mannone
 Kolo Toure
 Junichi Inamoto
 Igors Stepanovs
 Christopher Wreh

 Jehad Muntasser
 Tomas Danilevicius
 Carlos Vela
 Marouane Chamakh
 Kanu
 Pal Lydersen
 Lukasz Fabianski

 Luis Boa Morte
 Andrey Arshavin
 Armand Traore
 Daniel Le Roux
 Ju Young Park
 Jose Antonio Reyes
 Anders Limpar

 Philippe Senderos

 Emmanuel Adebayor
 Justin Hoyte

 Oguzhan Ozyakup
 Oleg Luzhny

 Danny Karbassiyoon

 Vladimir Petrovic

**38 SENEGAL (1)**
Armand Traore

**33 NIGERIA (1)**
Kanu
**34 NORWAY (1)**
Pal Lydersen
**35 POLAND (2)**
Lukasz Fabianski
Wojciech Szczesny
**36 PORTUGAL (3)**
Luis Boa Morte
Amaury Bischoff
Rui Fonte
**37 RUSSIA (1)**
Andrey Arshavin

**39 SOUTH AFRICA (1)**
Daniel Le Roux
**40 SOUTH KOREA (1)**
Ju Young Park
**41 SPAIN (9)**
Jose Antonio Reyes
Cesc Fabregas
Manuel Almunia
Fran Merida
Ignasi Miquel
Mikel Arteta
Santi Cazorla
Nacho Monreal
Hector Bellerin

**42 SWEDEN (7)**
Anders Limpar
Stefan Schwarz
Freddie Ljungberg
Rami Shaaban
Sebastian Larsson
Kristoffer Olsson
Kim Kallstrom
**43 SWITZERLAND (3)**
Philippe Senderos
Johan Djourou
Martin Angha
**44 TOGO (1)**
Emmanuel Adebayor

**45 TRINIDAD & TOBAGO (1)**
Justin Hoyte
**46 TURKEY (1)**
Oguzhan Ozyakup
**47 UKRAINE (1)**
Oleg Luzhny

**48 USA (2)**
Frankie Simek
Danny Karbassiyoon
**49 YUGOSLAVIA (1)**
Vladimir Petrovic

# Arsenal 2015/16 Season Shirt Competition

Answer the following question correctly and you could win an Arsenal FC shirt signed by a first team player.

In which year did Arsenal move from Highbury to Emirates?

## A. 2006    B. 2001    C. 1996

Entry is by email only. Only one entry per contestant. Please enter AFC SHIRT followed by either A, B or C in the subject line of an email.

In the body of the email, please include your full name, address, postcode, email address and phone number and send to:

frontdesk@grangecommunications.co.uk

by Friday 25 March 2016.

Toby from Gloucestershire won last year's signed shirt competition and here he is sporting his grand prize.

## Terms and Conditions

These terms and conditions ("Terms and Conditions") set out the basis on which you can participate in the Arsenal 2015/16 Season Shirt Competition ("Competition"). By entering the Competition, you accept these Terms and Conditions in full. If you do not accept these Terms and Conditions, you should not enter the Competition and you will not be eligible to win the prize. Entry is by email only. • ELIGIBILITY: Entry is open to UK residents only. Only one entry per person is allowed. • If entrants are under 18, consent from a parent or guardian must be obtained prior to entry and the parent or guardian must agree to these Terms and Conditions in full. • Employees of The Arsenal Football Club Plc (company number 109244) ("Arsenal"), the Promoter or members of their immediate families are not eligible to enter the Competition. • Entry is by email only. No purchase is required to enter but you will require email and internet access to enter the Competition. No refund may be claimed for any expenses incurred relating to the use of an email account or internet connection for the purpose of entering the Competition. • PRIZE: There will be one prize of an Arsenal 2015/16 season football shirt signed by at least one player for Arsenal's first team (the "Prize"). The Prize is non-transferable and no cash alternative will be offered. • SELECTION OF WINNER: The winner will be picked at random from all eligible and correct entries received between the Start Date and the Closing Date. • The winner will be contacted using the contact details provided on entry within 72 hours of the Closing Date. If the winner cannot be contacted or does not respond to confirm details for delivery of the Prize within 21 days, an alternative winner will be selected at random from the remaining eligible and correct entries. • Unless otherwise notified to the winner, the Prize will be delivered to the winner within 30 days of confirmation of the winner's address for delivery of the Prize. • PUBLICITY AND PERSONAL DATA: If the winner is aged 18 or over, the winner agrees to take part in reasonable publicity relating to the Competition and the Promoter and Arsenal may use the winner's name and image and his/her comments relating to the Competition and/or the Prize for future promotional, marketing and publicity purposes in any media worldwide without notice and without any fee being paid. • Details of the winner's name and county will be available on request for one month after the Closing Date by writing to the Promoter (including providing a stamped self-addressed envelope) at the address set out below. • The Promoter will use entrants' personal details for the purposes of administering the Competition and awarding the Prize. The Promoter may also pass on entrants' details to Arsenal, who may use the details to contact entrants about Arsenal's products and services, in accordance with Arsenal's privacy policy, available at http://www.arsenal.com/privacy-policy. By entering the Competition, you are indicating your agreement to this unless you tell us otherwise. If you do not wish to be contacted or to receive marketing information, you can opt out at any time by emailing AFC STOP to frontdesk@grangecommunications.co.uk. • OTHER IMPORTANT INFORMATION: Entries must not be submitted through agents or third parties. No responsibility can be accepted for lost, delayed, incomplete, or for electronic entries or winning notifications that are not received or delivered (for any reason including as a consequence of communication or network failures). Any such entries will be deemed void. • The Promoter reserves the right to withdraw or amend the Competition or these Terms and Conditions if circumstances outside its reasonable control make this unavoidable. • Entries must be strictly in accordance with these Terms and Conditions. Any entry not in strict accordance with these Terms and Conditions will be deemed to be invalid and the Prize will not be awarded in respect of such entry. The Promoter reserves the right to verify the eligibility of any entrant and to exclude any entries which it believes to be invalid or in breach of these Terms and Conditions. • The Promoter's decision is final in all matters relating to the Competition (including the Prize) and no correspondence will be entered into. • Except in respect of death or personal injury resulting from any negligence of Arsenal, to the maximum extent permitted by law, neither Arsenal nor any of its officers, employees or agents shall be responsible for (whether in tort, contract or otherwise): • any loss, damage or injury to you and/or any third party or to any property belonging to you or any third party in connection with the Competition and/or the Prize (including the winner's receipt or use of the same), resulting from any cause whatsoever; or • any loss of profit, loss of use, loss of opportunity or any indirect, economic or consequential losses whatsoever and howsoever caused. • GOVERNING LAW AND JURISDICTION: The Competition, and any dispute or claim arising out of or in connection with it, shall be governed by and construed in accordance with English law. You irrevocably agree that the courts of England and Wales shall have exclusive jurisdiction to settle any dispute or claim that arises out of or in connection with the Competition. • SPIRIT OF THE COMPETITION: If you attempt to compromise the integrity or proper operation of the Competition by cheating or committing fraud in any way, the Promoter and Arsenal each reserve the right to render your entry invalid, seek damages from you and ban you from participating in any of their future competitions. • CONTACT: If you have any questions about the Competition, please contact the Promoter. • PROMOTER: The Promoter of the Competition is Grange Communications Ltd, 22 Great King Street, Edinburgh EH3 6QH ("Promoter") on behalf of Arsenal.

# Spot the Difference

Can you work out the ten differences between the two pictures below? Answers on p61.

# On This Day...

Did Arsenal win a trophy on the day you were bo
Do you share your birthday with a Gunners leg
Take a look below and find out!

## January

1. Jack Wilshere was born (1992)
2. Ian Wright scored a hat-trick against Yeovil (1993)
3. Ryo Miyaichi signed (2011)
4. Arsenal beat Tottenham 2-0 in the FA Cup (2014)
5. Steve Walford was born (1958)
6. Arsenal beat Liverpool 3-1 in the FA Cup (2007)
7. Malcolm McDonald was born (1950)
8. Arsenal beat Tottenham 3-0 in the FA Cup (1949)
9. Thierry Henry scored in his comeback game against Leeds United (2012)
10. Marouane Chamakh was born (1984)
11. Brian Talbot signed (1979)
12. Thierry Henry scored his 100th Arsenal goal (2003)
13. Abou Diaby signed (2006)
14. Arsenal beat Middlesbrough 7-0 at Highbury (2006)
15. Kanu signed (1999)
16. Nicklas Bendtner was born (1988)
17. Manchester United v Arsenal set attendance record of 83,260 (1948)
18. Johan Djourou was born (1987)
19. Legendary manager Herbert Chapman was born (1878)
20. Theo Walcott signed (2006)
21. Thierry Henry scored a last-minute winner against Manchester United (2007)
22. Arsenal v Sheffield United was the first-ever game broadcast live on the radio (1927)
23. Alan Skirton was born (1939)
24. Gedion Zelalem made his debut aged 16 (2014)
25. Arsenal played as the 'away' side against Farnborough at Highbury (2003)
26. Gedion Zelalem was born (1997)
27. Yaya Sanogo was born (1993)
28. Gabriel signed (2015)
29. Ray Parlour made his debut v Liverpool (1992)
30. Arsenal beat Manchester United 5-0 in the FA Cup (1937)
31. Nacho Monreal signed (2013)

**5 JAN**

**19 JAN**

**25 JAN**

## February

1. Hector Bellerin scored his first goal (2015)
2. Former Ladies captain Faye White was bor (1978)
3. Arsenal beat Leeds 3-2 in the FA Cup (1993
4. Thierry Henry scored his 200th Arsenal goa (2006)
5. Giovanni van Bronckhorst was born (1975)
6. Arsenal beat West Ham 4-0 away (1999)
7. Arsenal beat Everton 1-0 in the first-leg of the League Cup semi-final (1988)
8. Carl Jenkinson was born (1992)
9. Paul Mariner signed (1984)
10. Arsenal beat Everton 1-0 to start 13-match winning streak (2002)
11. Thierry Henry scored his 228th and final goal for Arsenal (2012)
12. Joe Baker played his final game for the Gunners (1966)
13. Liam Brady was born (1956)
14. Arsenal beat France 2-0 in a friendly match at Highbury (1989)
15. Arsenal beat Manchester United 2-0 at Old Trafford in the FA Cup (2003)
16. Arsenal beat Barcelona 2-1 at Emirates Stadium (2011)
17. Jimmy Ashcroft became Arsenal's first England international (1906)
18. Tony Adams made his England debut v Spain (1987)
19. Arsenal beat Chelsea 2-0 at Highbury (1938)
20. Nicolas Anelka scored a hat-trick as Arsena beat Leicester City 5-0 (1999)
21. Arsenal beat Real Madrid 1-0 in the Champions League at the Bernabeu (2006)
22. Arsenal beat Manchester City 5-1 at Maine Road (2003)
23. Nicolas Anelka signed (1997)
24. Legendary midfielder George Armstrong made his debut (1962)
25. Theo Walcott scored his first Arsenal goal (2007)
26. Arsenal beat Tottenham 5-2 in the Premier League (2012)
27. Arsenal beat Bayer Leverkusen 4-1 in the Champions League (2002)
28. Robert Pires scored his 50th Arsenal goal (2004)
29. Thomas Shanks scored a hat-trick in a 4-0 win over Burnley (1904)

**1 FEB**

**13 FEB**

**25 FEB**

# March

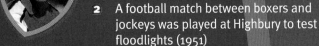
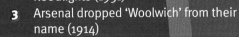

1 Arsenal beat Tottenham 2-1 away in the League Cup semi-final (1987)
2 Dennis Bergkamp scored a wonder-goal against Newcastle (2002)
3 Sylvain Wiltord scored a hat-trick v West Ham (2001)
4 Arsenal reached the Littlewoods Cup final after beating Tottenham (1987)
5 Ian Wright scored a hat-trick in 5-1 win v Ipswich (1994)
6 Arsenal beat Tottenham 6-0 at White Hart Lane (1935)
7 Ray Parlour was born (1973)

**7 MAR**

8 Arsenal knocked Real Madrid out of the Champions League (2006)
9 Highbury's record attendance of 73,295 was set v Sunderland (1935)
10 Arsenal beat Crystal Palace to reach the final of the Coca-Cola Cup (1993)
11 Arsenal beat Roma on penalties in the Champions League (2009)
12 Arsenal recorded their record league win - 12-0 against Loughborough Town (1900)
13 Former Arsenal manager George Allison passed away (1957)
14 Cliff Bastin was born (1912)

**17 MAR**

15 Arsenal lost the League Cup final to Swindon (1969)
16 Goalkeeper Frank Moss scored in 2-0 win over Everton (1935)
17 Lee Dixon was born (1964)
18 Arsenal beat Dinamo Bacau 7-1 in the European Fairs Cup (1970)
19 Hector Bellerin was born (1995)
20 Jock Rutherford became Arsenal's oldest ever player, aged 41 years and 159 days (1926)
21 John Radford made his debut (1964)
22 Arsenal beat Chelsea to reach the FA Cup final (1950)

**31 MAR**

23 Ray Parlour scored a hat-trick against Werder Bremen (2000)
24 Anders Limpar left Arsenal for Everton (1994)
25 Brian Marwood signed (1988)
26 Mikel Arteta was born (1982)
27 Arsenal drew 2-2 with Stoke in the FA Cup semi-final (1971)
28 Arsenal beat Juventus 2-0 in the Champions League (2006)
29 Marc Overmars was born (1973)
30 Arsenal and Manchester United (then Newton Heath) met for the first time (1895)
31 Legendary midfielder David Rocastle died (2001)

# April

![Arsenal]

1 Abou Diaby scored his first Arsenal goal (2006)
2 A football match between boxers and jockeys was played at Highbury to test floodlights (1951)
3 Arsenal dropped 'Woolwich' from their name (1914)
4 Arsenal beat Tottenham 1-0 in the FA Cup semi-final (1993)
5 Arsenal beat Liverpool 2-1 in the Littlewoods Cup final (1987)
6 Arsenal beat Tottenham 2-1 at Highbury (2002)
7 Paul Davis made his debut (1980)
8 Mikel Arteta scored in a 1-0 win over Manchester City (2012)
9 Thierry Henry scored a hat-trick as Arsenal beat Liverpool 4-2 (2004)
10 Arsenal won the league title with 1-1 draw at Huddersfield (1948)
11 Paul Merson scored his only Arsenal hat-trick (1992)
12 Silvinho was born (1974)

**1 APR**

13 Arsenal beat Blackburn 4-1 at Ewood Park (1998)
14 Arsenal beat Middlesbrough 1-0 in the FA Cup semi-final (2002)
15 Dennis Bergkamp scored his 120th and final Arsenal goal (2006)
16 Freddie Ljungberg was born (1977)
17 Jack Wilshere was named PFA Young Player of the Season (2011)

**12 APR**

18 Arsenal beat Sheffield Wednesday to win the League Cup (1993)
19 Arsenal beat Villarreal to reach the Champions League final (2006)
20 Arsenal beat Lens to reach UEFA Cup final (2000)
21 Andrey Arshavin scored four in a 4-4 draw at Liverpool (2009)

**21 APR**

22 Arsenal won the league title with a 3-1 victory at Chelsea (1933)
23 Arsenal beat Juventus 1-0 to reach the final of the European Cup Winners' Cup (1980)
24 Arsenal won 6-1 away to Middlesbrough (1999)
25 Arsenal beat Sheffield United in the FA Cup final (1936)
26 Arsenal won their first-ever FA Cup (1930)
27 Thierry Henry was named PFA Player of the Year (2003)

**30 APR**

28 Arsenal won the European Fairs Cup Final (1970)
29 Arsenal beat Liverpool 2-0 in the FA Cup final (1950)
30 Ray Kennedy and Bob Wilson played their last Arsenal games (1974)

# On This Day...

## May

1 Arsenal beat Burnley 3-2 to win the league title (1953)
2 David Rocastle was born (1967)
3 Arsenal beat Everton 4-0 to win the Premier League (1998)
4 Arsenal beat Parma 1-0 in the Cup Winners' Cup final (1994)
5 Arsenal beat Bolton 2-1 to secure European football on the last day of the season (1996)
6 Arsenal were crowned league champions for the tenth time (1991)
7 The final ever match at Highbury was a 4-2 win against Wigan (2006)
8 Arsenal clinched the Premier League at Old Trafford (2002)
9 Viv Anderson played his last game for Arsenal (1987)
10 Dennis Bergkamp was born (1969)
11 Arsenal wore red and white for the final time at Highbury (2005)
12 Arsenal beat Manchester United 3-2 to win the FA Cup final (1979)
13 Francis Coquelin was born (1991)
14 George Graham was appointed Arsenal manager (1986)
15 The unbeaten league season was completed with victory over Leicester (2004)
16 Arsenal beat Newcastle 2-0 in the FA Cup final (1998)
17 Arsenal beat Hull City to win the FA Cup for the 11th time (2014)
18 Arsenal completed the season with 3-2 win over Sheffield Wednesday (1963)
19 Manuel Almunia was born (1977)
20 Arsenal won the FA Cup final replay against Sheffield Wednesday (1993)
21 Arsenal won the FA Cup final on penalties against Manchester United (2005)
22 Robin van Persie scored for the ninth consecutive Premier League away game (2011)
23 Tomas Rosicky signed (2006)
24 Vito Mannone made his debut (2009)
25 Arsenal played a friendly match against Vasco de Gama while on tour in Brazil (1949)
26 Arsenal won the league title with a late 2-0 win at Anfield (1989)
27 Gervinho was born (1987)
28 Oleg Luzhny signed (1999)
29 Andrey Arshavin was born (1981)
30 Lauren signed (2000)
31 Alan Sunderland won his only England cap (1980)

**13 MAY**

**22 MAY**

**24 MAY**

**3 JUN**

**12 JUN**

**22 JUN**

## June

1 Arsenal Ladies won the FA Cup for the 13th time (2014)
2 Tom Whittaker appointed manager (1947)
3 Steve Bould signed (1988)
4 Lukas Podolski was born (1985)
5 The departures of Andrey Arshavin and Denilson were announced (2013)
6 Alex James appeared for the final time in an Arsenal shirt, in a friendly v Feyenoord (1937)
7 Arsenal played their only ever league fixture in the month of June, and lost 2-1 to Sheffield United (1947)
8 Carl Jenkinson signed (2011)
9 Dennis Bergkamp revealed his fear of flying (1998)
10 David Platt was born (1966)
11 Liam Brady joined as an apprentice (1971)
12 Pat Jennings was born (1945)
13 Aaron Ramsey signed (2008)
14 Emma Byrne was born (1979)
15 Bruce Rioch was appointed manager (1995)
16 Alex Manninger signed (1997)
17 Mathieu Debuchy signed (2014)
18 Paul Davis joined as an apprentice (1979)
19 Giovanni van Bronckhorst signed (2001)
20 Dennis Bergkamp signed (1995)
21 George Swindin was appointed manager (1958)
22 Charlie Nicholas signed (1983)
23 Patrick Vieira was born (1976)
24 Stefan Malz signed (1999)
25 Thierry Henry left Arsenal (2007)
26 Olivier Giroud signed (2012)
27 Arsenal's pre-season friendly against Rapid Vienna was abandoned due to crowd trouble (2002)
28 Arsenal officially took ownership of site in Highbury (1913)
29 Cesc Fabregas won the European Championships with Spain (2008)
30 Silvinho signed (1999)

# July

**9 JUL**

1 Lukas Podolski signed (2012)
2 Patrick Vieira, Thierry Henry and Emmanuel Petit won the European Championships with France (2000)
3 Sol Campbell signed (2001)
4 Dennis Bergkamp became Holland's record goalscorer (1998)
5 Richard Wright signed (2001)
6 Arsenal Ladies become the first Gunners side to play in a Puma kit (2014)
7 Laurent Koscielny signed (2010)
8 Sol Campbell left Arsenal (2006)
9 Terry Neill was appointed manager (1976)
10 Alexis Sanchez signed (2014)
11 Edu signed (2000)
12 Patrick Vieira and Emmanuel Petit won the World Cup with France (1998)

**14 JUL**

13 Mesut Ozil, Lukas Podolski and Per Mertesacker won the World Cup with Germany (2014)

**24 JUL**

14 Serge Gnabry was born (1995)
15 Patrick Vieira left Arsenal (2005)
16 John Hollins was born (1946)
17 Joe Baker was born (1940)
18 Gervinho signed (2011)

**31 JUL**

19 Aaron Ramsey appeared for Arsenal for the first time in a friendly against Barnet (2008)
20 Bob McNab was born (1943)
21 Brian Talbot was born (1953)
22 Dennis Bergkamp's testimonial was played at Emirates Stadium (2006)
23 Jon Sammels was born (1945)
24 Martin Keown was born (1966)
25 Jens Lehmann signed (2003)
26 Paul Merson joined the Arsenal youth system (1984)
27 David Ospina signed (2014)
28 Mathieu Debuchy was born (1985)
29 Viv Anderson was born (1956)
30 George Eastham won the World Cup with England (1966)
31 Arsenal drew 1-1 with New York Red Bulls in the Emirates Cup (2011)

# August

1 Arsenal won the Charity Shield against Manchester United (1999)
2 Arsenal beat Rangers 3-0 to win the Emirates Cup (2009)
3 Thierry Henry signed (1999)
4 Bryn Jones signed for a UK transfer record of £14,000 (1938)
5 Oleg Luzhny was born (1968)
6 Arsenal beat Independiente of Argentina 2-1 in Miami (1989)
7 Thierry Henry made his debut (1999)
8 Arsenal won the Charity Shield with a 3-1 win over Manchester United (2004)
9 Arsenal beat Manchester United 3-0 to win the Charity Shield (1998)
10 Arsenal shared the Charity Shield with Tottenham (1991)
11 Jack Wilshere made his England debut (2010)
12 Kenny Sansom signed for Arsenal (1980)
13 Aaron Ramsey made his Arsenal debut (2008)
14 Patrick Vieira signed (1996)
15 Arsenal's first-ever Premier League match ended in defeat to Norwich (1992)
16 Arsenal beat Tottenham 1-0 away (1993)
17 Thierry Henry was born (1977)
18 Santi Cazorla made his debut (2012)
19 The first game at Emirates Stadium was a 1-1 draw with Aston Villa (2006)
20 Dennis Bergkamp made his debut (1995)
21 Theo Walcott scored his first Arsenal hat-trick (2010)
22 Arsenal equalled the record for 42 league games unbeaten (2004)
23 Arsenal won their first game at Emirates Stadium (2006)
24 Vic Akers was born (1946)
25 David Seaman made his debut (1990)
26 Arsenal beat Charlton 5-3 at Highbury (2000)
27 Dennis Bergkamp scored an incredible hat-trick against Leicester (1997)
28 Alex Oxlade-Chamberlain made his Arsenal debut (2011)
29 Mathieu Flamini joined for the second time (2013)
30 Alf Baker made his debut (1919)
31 Per Mertesacker and Mikel Arteta signed (2011)

**5 AUG**

**24 AUG**

**25 AUG**

# On This Day...

## September

**1** Jose Antonio Reyes was born (1983)

**2** Woolwich Arsenal's first-ever league game ended in a 2-2 draw with Newcastle United (1893)

**3** Brazil beat Argentina in the first international at Emirates Stadium (2006)

**4** Arsenal beat Leeds 7-0 in the League Cup (1979)

**5** Percy Sands made his Arsenal debut (1903)

**6** The first match at Highbury ended in a 2-1 win over Leicester Fosse (1913)

**7** Peter Storey was born (1945)

**8** Arsenal beat Liverpool 3-1 at Highbury (1984)

**9** The club played their first-ever away league match (1893)

**10** Laurent Koscielny was born (1985)

**11** Laurent Koscielny scored his first Arsenal goal (2010)

**12** Freddie Ljungberg signed (1998)

**13** Ian Wright broke the club goalscoring record (1997)

**14** Mesut Ozil made his Arsenal debut (2013)

**15** Arsenal beat Tottenham 3-1 away (2007)

**16** Arsenal's first ever Champions League match ended 1-1 with Lens (1998)

**17** Arsenal won 1-0 away to Manchester United (2006)

**18** Thierry Henry scored his first Arsenal goal (1999)

**19** David Seaman was born (1963)

**20** Freddie Ljungberg scored on his debut (1998)

**21** Arsenal beat Tottenham 4-1 in the Carling Cup at White Hart Lane (2010)

**22** Emmanuel Petit was born (1970)

**23** Ian Wright signed (1991)

**24** Anders Limpar was born (1965)

**25** Hector Bellerin made his debut (2013)

**26** Arsenal won the Charity Shield (1938)

**27** Freddie Ljungberg scored twice as Arsenal beat Lazio 2-0 in the Champions League (2000)

**28** Alan Skirton became Arsenal's first ever substitute (1965)

**29** Per Mertesacker was born (1984)

**30** Arsenal beat Panathinaikos 2-1 in the first Wembley Champions League game (1998)

**7 SEP**

**11 SEP**

**22 SEP**

**1 OCT**

**15 OCT**

**25 OCT**

## October

**1** Arsène Wenger was appointed Arsenal manager (1996)

**2** Arsenal beat Barnet 5-2 in the 75th anniversary match (1962)

**3** Michael Thomas scored a hat-trick against Plymouth (1989)

**4** Tomas Rosicky was born (1980)

**5** Arsenal became the first English club to pla[y] in Russia (1954)

**6** Liam Brady made his debut (1973)

**7** Gilberto was born (1976)

**8** Arsenal won the Charity Shield (1930)

**9** Arsenal beat Manchester United in the Mercantile Credit final (1988)

**10** Tony Adams was born (1966)

**11** Arsenal beat Coventry City 5-0 (1975)

**12** Arsène Wenger took charge of his first matc[h] (1996)

**13** David Jack signed (1928)

**14** Woolwich Arsenal beat Ashford United 12-0 in the FA Cup (1893)

**15** Mesut Ozil was born (1988)

**16** Arsenal reach 49 consecutive games unbeaten in the league (2004)

**17** Jimmy Brain scored a hat-trick against Cardiff (1925)

**18** Arsenal won the Charity Shield (1933)

**19** Jack Wilshere scored his first Champions League goal (2010)

**20** Ted Drake scored a hat-trick against Tottenham (1934)

**21** Aaron Ramsey scored his first Arsenal goal (2008)

**22** Arsène Wenger was born (1949)

**23** Kanu scored a hat-trick in 3-2 win at Chelsea (1999)

**24** Arsenal beat Manchester City 3-0 away (2010)

**25** Pat Rice made his final appearance (1980)

**26** Arsène Wenger recorded his first home win (1996)

**27** Doug Lishman scored a hat-trick against Fulham at Highbury (1951)

**28** Cesc Fabregas became Arsenal's youngest ever player (2003)

**29** Robert Pires was born (1973)

**30** Arsenal beat Reading 7-5 in the League Cup (2012)

**31** Arsenal beat Tottenham 3-0 at Emirates Stadium (2009)

# November

1   Rachel Yankey was born (1979)
2   Alan Sunderland signed (1977)
3   Ian Wright was born (1963)
4   Dennis Bergkamp scored as Arsenal beat Manchester United 1-0 (1995)
5   Tony Adams made his debut (1983)
6   Arsenal beat Borrusia Dortmund 1-0 away (2014)
7   Arsenal beat Manchester City 5-2 (1925)
8   Arsenal beat Tottenham 2-1 at Highbury (2003)
9   Arsenal beat Manchester United 3-2 at Highbury (1997)
10  Jens Lehmann was born (1969)
11  Gilles Grimandi was born (1970)
12  Arsenal beat Liverpool 3-0 (2006)
13  Arsenal won 5-4 away to Tottenham (2004)
14  Seven Arsenal players were in the England side which beat Italy at Highbury (1934)
15  Arsenal recorded their biggest win at Anfield – 5-1 (1952)
16  Steve Bould was born (1962)
17  Per Mertesacker scored his first Arsenal goal (2012)
18  George Eastham signed (1960)
19  Jack Kelsey was born (1929)
20  Arsenal beat Tottenham in the League Cup semi-final at Highbury (1968)
21  Nigel Winterburn made his debut (1987)
22  Paul Merson made his league debut (1986)
23  Ian Wright scored for the 12th game in succession (1994)
24  Ted Drake scored four in a 5-2 win over Chelsea (1934)
25  Arsenal beat Inter Milan 5-1 at the San Siro (2003)
26  Danny Welbeck and Gabriel were both born (1990)
27  Thierry Henry scored a hat-trick away to Roma (2002)
28  Arsenal won the Charity Shield (1934)
29  David Jack scored a hat-trick as Arsenal beat Chelsea 5-1 (1930)
30  George Graham was born (1944)

**1 NOV**

**5 NOV**

**10 NOV**

**25 NOV**

# December

1   Ted Drake scored four as Arsenal beat Wolves 7-0 (1934)
2   Cesc Fabregas became Arsenal's youngest goalscorer (2003)
3   Arsenal beat Manchester United 1-0 (1989)
4   Arsenal beat Tottenham for the first time (1909)
5   Boro Primorac was born (1954)
6   Tony Woodcock was born (1955)
7   Patrick Vieira scored his first Arsenal goal (1996)
8   Ladies star Jordan Nobbs was born (1992)
9   Ainsley Maitland-Niles made his debut (2014)
10  Highbury's West Stand opened by HRH Prince of Wales (1932)
11  The club, as Dial Square, played their first ever match (1886)
12  Arsenal suffered their record defeat, 8-0 to Loughborough Town (1896)
13  Santi Cazorla was born (1984)
14  Ted Drake scored a record seven goals in a game (1935)
15  Arsenal beat Leicester 8-0 with hat-tricks from Ted Drake and Joe Hulme (1934)
16  Don Howe became Arsenal manager (1983)
17  Raphael Meade scored a hat-trick against Watford (1983)
18  Ronnie Rooke scored a hat-trick against Huddersfield (1948)
19  Alexis Sanchez was born (1988)
20  Arsenal beat Leeds 3-1 (1998)
21  Ian Wright scored four against Everton (1991)
22  Alan Ball signed (1971)
23  Arsenal beat Tottenham 5-0 (1978)
24  Arsenal smashed Sheffield United 9-2 (1932)
25  In a meeting at the Royal Oak Pub, the club's name was changed to Royal Arsenal (1886)
26  Aaron Ramsey was born (1990)
27  Arsenal beat Chelsea 3-1 at Emirates Stadium (2010)
28  Frank McLintock was born (1939)
29  Arsenal beat Newcastle 7-3 at Emirates Stadium (2012)
30  Charlie Nicholas was born (1961)
31  John Jensen scored his only Arsenal goal (1994)

**5 DEC**

**16 DEC**

**28 DEC**

# Schooldays

We asked our players to cast their minds back to when they were at school, here's what they told us.

**Koscielny:** I really loved mathematics because I liked working with numbers.

$$-5(4$$
$$(4x - (2 - 5y + 2x) + 2y)$$
$$\frac{(x-1)}{6} = \frac{(x+5)}{5}$$

**Giroud:** It was history, and I liked geography too. I'm really interested in history, especially the history of the wars.

for wh...
to be best in an...
point of view.
**History**...
events of the p...
past develop...
information...

## What was your favourite subject, not including PE?

**Chambers:** Design and technology. It's different to other subjects - you get to make and experiment with things.

**Coquelin:** I liked French literature and English. I was good at languages. I also liked German.

**Chambers:** Maybe a couple of times for handing homework in late. I wasn't that bad though, I didn't get many detentions.

**Giroud:** I only really got it once, when I got in a fight. But it wasn't my fault - I was just defending myself!

I must not fight in school
I must not fight in school
I must not fight in school
I must not fight in school
I must not fight in school
I must not fight in school
I must not fight in school

## How often did you get detention at school?

**Oxlade-Chamberlain:** I can remember one time. We used to do a sponsored walk round Queen Elizabeth Country Park to raise money for charity. One year a group of me and my friends decided to go off track. We got lost, didn't get to the checkpoints and we got caught. So they had us in over the summer holidays working with the maintenance men!

**Walcott:** Never. At primary school I had an incident when I had to stand against the wall for five minutes because someone nicked my ball and I reacted. But that was the only incident I ever had.

**Koscielny:** I was a striker when I was younger - I moved further back on the pitch the older I got. Maybe in a few years I will be a goalkeeper! But because I was a striker, I really liked Jean Pierre Papin of Marseille.

 **Which footballer did you pretend to be in the playground?**

**Wilshere:** It was David Beckham.

**Welbeck:** The players that people idolised in the playground back then were Ryan Giggs and Thierry Henry. They were my favourite players.

**Coquelin:** After 1998 everyone pretended to be Zidane. Actually when I was eight or nine I got an Arsenal shirt for Christmas. It's the old SEGA shirt, with my name on the back. I still have it today.

**Ramsey:** My thing was trying to get in to all of the sports teams so I could miss the other lessons! It was cricket, athletics, rugby, football, cross-country. Basically anything that was available.

**Welbeck:** I liked tennis. We had four tennis courts so I played a bit.

**Walcott:** I enjoyed the 100 metres and 200 metres, so sportsdays were always fun. But cricket will always stand out too. We had a good cricket team and I was a bit of an all-rounder, a slogger and not a bad bowler. I enjoyed cricket a lot because we went to other schools and were away for the whole day.

 **Did you play any other sports or activities apart from football?**

**Wilshere:** Yes, a few. I liked rugby. Also, for about two weeks I wanted to learn the piano, but I was so bad my mum said I had to stop. She said I was wasting her money!

# Wise Words

Can you match these Arsène Wenger quotes to the player?

**Mesut Ozil**

**1**
"He is a guy who has a good combination of talent, combative aspect and fighting spirit. Sometimes he is too demanding with himself."

**Patrick Vieira**

**2**
"For 20 years, until the last minute, he never made a pass in training without thinking about it, or without putting every part of his brain into it. That's something that I consider virtually impossible."

**Thierry Henry**

**3**
"The first I saw him play, he was 17 years of age, and he dominated the midfield. Straight away after the game I said 'this guy will make a great career'"

**4**
"What he does is always classy and intelligent. The timing of his passes is fantastic. You'd love to play with him."

**Alexis Sanchez**

**5**
"He is an Arsenal man. Certainly one day he will come back here. In what role I don't know."

**Dennis Bergkamp**

Check your answers on p61.

34

# Road to Wembley

Arsenal have won more FA Cups than any other side, but are you top of the class when it comes to FA Cup knowledge? Answer at least two questions correctly in each round to progress, but be warned! The closer you get to Wembley, the harder the questions become!

## THIRD ROUND

1. What colour shirts did Arsenal wear in the 2015 FA Cup final?
2. At which stadium was last season's final played?
3. What score did Arsenal beat Aston Villa in last season's final?

## FOURTH ROUND

1. How many home games did Arsenal play in the 2015 FA Cup?
2. Which team did Arsenal beat in the FA Cup semi-final in 2015?
3. Who scored Arsenal's last goal in the final last season?

## FIFTH ROUND

1. How many times has Arsène Wenger won the FA Cup?
2. Who did Arsenal beat in the 2005 FA Cup final?
3. Who scored a free-kick in the 2014 FA Cup final?

## QUARTER-FINAL

1. In which year did Arsène Wenger first win the FA Cup?
2. Name one of Arsenal's penalty takers in the 2014 semi-final win.
3. Who scored the winning goal in last season's quarter-final against Manchester United?

## SEMI-FINAL

1. In which minute did Theo Walcott open the scoring in last season's FA Cup final?
2. Who scored for Arsenal in both the 2001 and 2002 FA Cup finals?
3. How many FA Cup finals have Arsenal played in?

## FINAL

1. Who was the referee in last season's FA Cup final?
2. To the nearest 100, what was the attendance in last season's FA Cup final?
3. Who is Arsenal's all-time leading goalscorer in FA Cup matches?

 Now turn to p61 to see if you will lift the cup!

# Young Guns

There's plenty of exciting talent emerging from the youth system at Arsenal, these three youngsters will all hope to make their first-team debuts soon.

## Daniel Crowley

**Position: Midfielder**
**Born: Coventry, Aug 3, 1997**
**Signed pro: August 2014**

Likened in style and attitude to a young Jack Wilshere, Daniel frequently catches the eye operating in the number 10 role. He played 32 times for the various age groups at Arsenal last season, scoring 11 goals. Formerly part of the Aston Villa set-up, Daniel is now in his third season with the Gunners, and is a talisman within the academy. A set-piece specialist, the England youth international is a creator as well as scorer of goals, and likes to get on the ball as much as possible. Naturally high in confidence, Daniel often joins in first-team training sessions, and continues to develop his skills at an impressive rate.

# Alex Iwobi

**Position:** Forward
**Born:** Lagos, Nigeria, May 3, 1996
**Signed pro:** May 2014

As the nephew of former Nigeria great Jay Jay Okocha, football is in the blood for Alex Iwobi, and the young Gunner certainly has much in common with his famous relative. Okocha was known for his extensive repertoire of tricks, and Alex has skill to burn too. Captain of the side which played in the Champions Youth League last season, attacker Alex led by example as the side progressed through the group stage. He scored 11 goals overall at youth level last term, including a fantastic hat-trick at Emirates Stadium against Stoke City in the Under-21 Premier League in April. Although born in Nigeria, Alex has frequently represented England at youth level.

# Jon Toral

**Position:** Midfielder
**Born:** Reus, Spain, Feb 5, 1995
**Signed pro:** Feb 2012

Jon joined Arsenal from the Barcelona system at the same time as Hector Bellerin, and he will be hoping to follow his close friend and compatriot into the Gunners first team as soon as possible. A technically gifted wideman who possesses exceptional dribbling ability, Jon spent last season on loan in the Championship with Brentford, and helped fire the Bees all the way to the play-offs, with six goals from 34 league outings. The highlight of his loan spell was undoubtedly a fine hat-trick against Blackpool in February. Although a youth international with Spain, Jon is also eligible to represent England, through his mother.

# A Day in the Life of Colin Lewin

## Ever wondered what matchday is like for our first-team physiotherapist?

" For a Saturday 3pm game we stay in the team hotel the night before; at 10am I ring round every room to wake the players up.

We meet downstairs at 10.30 where the players have a chat and a drink. That's followed by a meeting and a team walk, and then we have the pre-match meal, about four hours before kick off.

By midday they have finished lunch and then some players usually come and see me or the massage therapists for treatment.

A couple of players might come and see me to check a stiff ankle or stiff back for example.

Then we pack up our equipment, get changed into our matchday suits and board the team bus to the stadium.

We leave at 1pm to get to the stadium for 1.40pm. The rest of the medical staff will already be there. For home matches we have two or three physios, two masseurs and Dr Gary O'Driscoll.

Shad Forsythe, the fitness coach, takes care of the warm-up with Steve Bould, which is 35 minutes before kick-off. While they are doing that I prepare my run-on bag. Basically it's packed with first aid equipment – lots of stuff that you hope you never use – but equally you don't want to get to the pitch without a pair of scissors, strappings or tape, or equipment that will stop bleeding for example. The main equipment like stretchers, defibrillator, gasses, etc., is positioned pitchside with the doctor and paramedics.

During the match I'm obviously prepared to be called on by the ref at any point. I can't enter the field until instructed by the referee, even if the player is down.

When I get on to the pitch, the most important thing in the initial 20 seconds or so is to work out whether they can continue or not. If I think they can, then I try to assess the injury a bit more.

If the player thinks he can continue, and we are happy with the assessment, then we do our best to patch them up and keep them on.

If a player does come off we can administer immediate treatment in the dressing room in the stadium and we also have X-ray facilities there too.

At the final whistle we head to the dressing room and the medical team do a quick spot check on those who played.

We have a cold bath at the Emirates and the players are encouraged to use that post-match in order to begin the recovery process as soon as possible.

Before we all head home I give the manager a summary of any problems, but the real crux of that chat happens the next day, with all the coaches.

Finally we tidy up and then have a debrief among the medical team, looking back on the game and ahead to the next few days.

# Search for... a (hat-trick) hero!

**All these players have scored hat-tricks for Arsenal**

```
A R S H P A H W R E M E N W I L T O R D
D D H F W W O V E R M A R S O Z A E R L
E C E G E B E R O T P R O O R B A P E J
B E R B D C E S R K S A V S L A N H B U
A W C O A N E L K A V I R R A P E W J N
R B A L I Y B S D N W P E L H A L E P G
N I Z I V P O S W U E T R E O C S L A B
K N P I I A L R O Z A C M M E U A B R O
A O I S E H S G R W L N A G N P R E K C
E S A C E U O I I W A L C O T T B C A A
L R Z A M R J R G I L A R R R M B K M Z
K E Y I J K I O H L A N S E Y E E R P L
A M X A M E S P T S C N P B N A B O Y N
A P W E E E K U P K O T A D K K E Y Z I
R E J A V E L D G C T E T G A G N A K V
S N H E E L M S L E T N R H N R D B A A
H N S O J O N R A L E V L N G Y R N E H
W A L J U N G B E R G K A M P I T E N S
A N H E P T S R U B W P O U U E R D U R
A T S I T P A B Q L E R U J L B N W A A
```

| | | | |
|---|---|---|---|
| Adebayor | Bergkamp | Merson | Vela |
| Anelka | Cazorla | Overmars | Walcott |
| Arshavin | Henry | Parlour | Welbeck |
| Baptista | Kanu | Pennant | Wiltord |
| Bendtner | Ljungberg | Pires | Wright |

Answers on p61.

# Stat-attack

## Arsenal's all-time leading goalscorers and appearance makers

Thierry Henry

Peter Storey

## Top 10 all-time goalscorers

| | Player | Years played | Games | Goals | Games per goal |
|---|---|---|---|---|---|
| 1 | Thierry Henry | 1999-07 & 2012 | 228 | 377 | 1.65 |
| 2 | Ian Wright | 1991-98 | 185 | 288 | 1.56 |
| 3 | Cliff Bastin | 1929-46 | 178 | 396 | 2.22 |
| 4 | John Radford | 1964-76 | 149 | 482 | 3.23 |
| 5 | Jimmy Brain | 1924-31 | 139 | 232 | 1.67 |
| 6 | Ted Drake | 1934-39 | 139 | 184 | 1.32 |
| 7 | Doug Lishman | 1948-55 | 137 | 244 | 1.78 |
| 8 | Robin van Persie | 2004-12 | 132 | 278 | 2.11 |
| 9 | Joe Hulme | 1926-37 | 125 | 374 | 2.99 |
| 10 | David Jack | 1928-34 | 124 | 208 | 1.68 |

John Radford

Lee Dixon

## Top 10 all-time appearance-makers

| | Player | Years played | Starts | Subs | Total |
|---|---|---|---|---|---|
| 1 | David O'Leary | 1975-93 | 681 | 41 | 722 |
| 2 | Tony Adams | 1983-2002 | 663 | 6 | 669 |
| 3 | George Armstrong | 1962-77 | 607 | 14 | 621 |
| 4 | Lee Dixon | 1988-2002 | 598 | 21 | 619 |
| 5 | Nigel Winterburn | 1987-2000 | 572 | 12 | 584 |
| 6 | David Seaman | 1990-2003 | 564 | 0 | 564 |
| 7 | Pat Rice | 1967-80 | 521 | 7 | 528 |
| 8 | Peter Storey | 1965-77 | 494 | 7 | 501 |
| 9 | John Radford | 1964-76 | 476 | 6 | 482 |
| 10 | Peter Simpson | 1964-78 | 459 | 19 | 478 |

Peter Simpson

Nigel Winterburn

Robin van Persie

Pat Rice

David Seaman

# Arsène Wenger
## Coaching Masterclass

He's one of the most highly respected coaches in world football and here Arsène Wenger reveals how he teaches the players five of the essential techniques in football.

## Tackling

The secret is the timing of your intervention, the technique to go down with one leg and basically to put your body in the position of a hurdler. If you are a super tackler, you can make a pass when you win the ball with your intervention. That means you can take care again of the attacking side. That is the most important thing: to be calm and master well what you do. When a tackle is well timed, with a thought process behind it - I find it a marvellous technique that is under-rated in the game.

## Volleying

The secret is to really meet the ball with intention, look at the ball and have no hesitation. That means you fly away with the ball. It's a question of belief more than technique, because every single player can play a good volley. But if you have hesitancy, you will miss. The combination of concentration and belief that is behind a volley is the most interesting aspect, more than the technical side, because all players can do that. At the top level though the difference is they do it eight times out of ten, not once out of ten!

# Crossing

A cross has to be an assist, which means it is the final ball. When you make a cross, nobody other than your forward should touch it in front of goal. Too many people get into the habit of crossing the ball just thinking, 'I hope somebody will be on the end of it'. When I was young, my coach told me that wasn't a cross. A cross is a final pass and a final pass has to be perfect. A good cross can also sometimes be a cut back. Defenders run against their goal and you know that you have midfielders who can arrive at the right time in the box.

# Passing

A quality pass is something that makes the circulation fluid. For that it demands technical ability of course, it demands intelligence and it demands a generous attitude. I'm a big lover of the pass, but I'm also a big lover of the timing of the pass. If someone delays a pass, even if they make a good pass, they are giving the next guy in possession less time. All the aspects have to be right: the moment of the decision and the quality of the pass.

# Heading

It's a question of timing your jump, protection, and then timing the header. A good technique is to head the ball while your body is completely vertical. Some players jump up with their elbows out, protecting them. The advantage is that when the guy next to you jumps, as long as you jump first, he lifts you up. The other advantage is that when you head the ball early, the force is straight. When you hit it with your forehead, you can direct it better. Most players head the ball too early, and it comes off the top of their head.

# The Mesut Ozil Quiz

**He's one of the best players in the world, but how well do you know Arsenal's number 11?**

**1.** Which club did Arsenal sign Mesut from?

**2.** Which make of boots does he wear?

**3.** In which year did he win the World Cup for Germany?

**4.** Who did he make his Arsenal debut against?

**5.** True or false, Mesut was named in the UEFA Team of the Year in both 2012 and 2013?

**6.** Name one of the two Bundesliga clubs he played for.

**7.** In which year was he born?

**8.** How many assists did he get last season? 6 or 9?

**9.** Is Mesut left-footed or right-footed?

**10.** As well as Germany, which other country was Mesut eligible to play for?

**11.** Who is Mesut scoring a free-kick against last season in this picture?

Answers on p61.

# Quiz
## Name the Season

How good is your memory? Take a look at these five pictures, use the clues, and fill in the season for each one! Answers are on p61.

**1**
**Top scorer:** Alan Smith
**League position:** 1st
**Season:**

**Top scorer:** Dennis Bergkamp
**League position:** 1st
**Season:**
**2**

**3**
**Top scorer:** Thierry Henry
**League position:** 1st
**Season:**

**Top scorer:** Thierry Henry
**League position:** 4th
**Season:**
**4**

**5**
**Top scorer:** Robin van Persie
**League position:** 3rd
**Season:**

# Junior Gunners

## Become a Junior Gunner

Junior Gunners is Arsenal's youth membership scheme for fans up to 16 years old. As a JG you get to have loads of fun with the club you love; ranging from events for your whole family to fun competitions on the @Gunnersaurus and @JuniorGunners twitter accounts.

**Some of the best things about being a JG...**

* Discounted match tickets.
* Exclusive events, such as trips to London Colney and family fun days.
* Fun competitions, with prizes such as signed items and match tickets.
* Chances to be a matchday mascot and part of the ball squad.
* 10 per cent off Arsenal Soccer Schools courses.
* A FREE stadium tour voucher*.
* A cool Membership pack*.

There are three tiers of JG membership; Welcome to our World (birth to three years), Team JGs (four to 11) and Young Guns (12 to 16). Each tier can enjoy their own events and competitions.

To find out more, head to:

**alwaysaheadofthegame.com/junior.**

*Full Membership Only.

# Quiz Solutions

## P.20 True or False

| | | | |
|---|---|---|---|
| 1. | False | 6. | True |
| 2. | True | 7. | False |
| 3. | True | 8. | True |
| 4. | False | 9. | False |
| 5. | True | 10. | False |

## P.21 Odd One Out

1. Johan Djourou (the others are French)
2. Philippe Senderos (the others are goalkeepers)
3. Theo Walcott (the others are Invincibles)
4. 2009 (the others are FA Cup-winning seasons)
5. Tottenham (the others Arsenal faced in last season's FA Cup)
6. Alan Smith (the others are Arsenal managers)
7. Lee Dixon (the others all wore no.10)
8. Golden Gantry (the others are places at Emirates Stadium)

## P.25 Spot The Difference

## P.34 Wise Words

1. Alexis Sanchez
2. Dennis Bergkamp
3. Patrick Vieira
4. Mesut Ozil
5. Thierry Henry

## P.35 Road To Wembley

| | |
|---|---|
| Third Round. | 1. Yellow, 2. Wembley, 3. 4-0. |
| Fourth Round. | 1. Two, 2. Reading, 3. Olivier Giroud. |
| Fifth Round. | 1. Six, 2. Manchester United, 3. Santi Cazorla |
| Quarter-Final. | 1. 1998, 2. Mikel Arteta, Kim Kallstrom, Olivier Giroud or Santi Cazorla, 3. Danny Welbeck. |
| Semi-final. | 1. 40th, 2. Freddie Ljungberg, 3. 19. |
| Final. | 1. Jonathan Moss, 2. 89,283, 3. Cliff Bastin (26) |

## P.54 Wordsearch

| | | | |
|---|---|---|---|
| Adebayor | Bergkamp | Merson | Vela |
| Anelka | Cazorla | Overmars | Walcott |
| Arshavin | Henry | Parlour | Welbeck |
| Baptista | Kanu | Pennant | Wiltord |
| Bendtner | Ljungberg | Pires | Wright |

## P.58 The Mesut Ozil Quiz

| | | | |
|---|---|---|---|
| 1. | Real Madrid | 7. | 1988 |
| 2. | Adidas | 8. | 9 |
| 3. | 2014 | 9. | Left-footed |
| 4. | Sunderland | 10. | Turkey |
| 5. | True | 11. | Liverpool |
| 6. | Schalke, Werder Bremen | | |

## P.59 Name The Season

1. 1988/89
2. 1997/98
3. 2003/04
4. 2005/06
5. 2011/12

Where's Gunnersa